RENTAL LEDGER

THIS BOOK BELONGS TO:

NAME:

_____

_____

ADDRESS:

_____

_____

_____

PHONE:

_____

_____

RENTAL LEDGER BOOK

YEAR	
TENANT	
ADDRESS	
AMOUNT OF MONTHLY RENT	DATE DUE

MONTH	DAY RENT RECEIVED	AMOUNT RECEIVED	AMOUNT NOT RECEIVED	LATE FEES	COMMENTS
JANUARY					
FEBRUARY					
MARCH					
APRIL					
MAY					
JUNE					
JULY					
AUGUST					
SEPTEMBER					
OCTOBER					
NOVEMBER					
DECEMBER					
TOTALS					

NOTES

RENTAL LEDGER BOOK

YEAR	
TENANT	
ADDRESS	
AMOUNT OF MONTHLY RENT		DATE DUE	

MONTH	DAY RENT RECEIVED	AMOUNT RECEIVED	AMOUNT NOT RECEIVED	LATE FEES	COMMENTS
JANUARY					
FEBRUARY					
MARCH					
APRIL					
MAY					
JUNE					
JULY					
AUGUST					
SEPTEMBER					
OCTOBER					
NOVEMBER					
DECEMBER					
TOTALS					

NOTES

RENTAL LEDGER BOOK

YEAR	
TENANT	
ADDRESS	
AMOUNT OF MONTHLY RENT	DATE DUE

MONTH	DAY RENT RECEIVED	AMOUNT RECEIVED	AMOUNT NOT RECEIVED	LATE FEES	COMMENTS
JANUARY					
FEBRUARY					
MARCH					
APRIL					
MAY					
JUNE					
JULY					
AUGUST					
SEPTEMBER					
OCTOBER					
NOVEMBER					
DECEMBER					
TOTALS					

NOTES

RENTAL LEDGER BOOK

YEAR	
TENANT	
ADDRESS	
AMOUNT OF MONTHLY RENT		DATE DUE	

MONTH	DAY RENT RECEIVED	AMOUNT RECEIVED	AMOUNT NOT RECEIVED	LATE FEES	COMMENTS
JANUARY					
FEBRUARY					
MARCH					
APRIL					
MAY					
JUNE					
JULY					
AUGUST					
SEPTEMBER					
OCTOBER					
NOVEMBER					
DECEMBER					
TOTALS					

NOTES

RENTAL LEDGER BOOK

YEAR	
TENANT	
ADDRESS	
AMOUNT OF MONTHLY RENT	

DATE DUE

MONTH	DAY RENT RECEIVED	AMOUNT RECEIVED	AMOUNT NOT RECEIVED	LATE FEES	COMMENTS
JANUARY					
FEBRUARY					
MARCH					
APRIL					
MAY					
JUNE					
JULY					
AUGUST					
SEPTEMBER					
OCTOBER					
NOVEMBER					
DECEMBER					
TOTALS					

NOTES

RENTAL LEDGER BOOK

YEAR	
TENANT	
ADDRESS	

AMOUNT OF MONTHLY RENT		DATE DUE	

MONTH	DAY RENT RECEIVED	AMOUNT RECEIVED	AMOUNT NOT RECEIVED	LATE FEES	COMMENTS
JANUARY					
FEBRUARY					
MARCH					
APRIL					
MAY					
JUNE					
JULY					
AUGUST					
SEPTEMBER					
OCTOBER					
NOVEMBER					
DECEMBER					
TOTALS					

NOTES

RENTAL LEDGER BOOK

YEAR	
TENANT	
ADDRESS	
AMOUNT OF MONTHLY RENT	DATE DUE

MONTH	DAY RENT RECEIVED	AMOUNT RECEIVED	AMOUNT NOT RECEIVED	LATE FEES	COMMENTS
JANUARY					
FEBRUARY					
MARCH					
APRIL					
MAY					
JUNE					
JULY					
AUGUST					
SEPTEMBER					
OCTOBER					
NOVEMBER					
DECEMBER					
TOTALS					

NOTES

RENTAL LEDGER BOOK

YEAR	
TENANT	
ADDRESS	
AMOUNT OF MONTHLY RENT	DATE DUE

MONTH	DAY RENT RECEIVED	AMOUNT RECEIVED	AMOUNT NOT RECEIVED	LATE FEES	COMMENTS
JANUARY					
FEBRUARY					
MARCH					
APRIL					
MAY					
JUNE					
JULY					
AUGUST					
SEPTEMBER					
OCTOBER					
NOVEMBER					
DECEMBER					
TOTALS					

NOTES

RENTAL LEDGER BOOK

YEAR	
TENANT	
ADDRESS	
AMOUNT OF MONTHLY RENT	DATE DUE

MONTH	DAY RENT RECEIVED	AMOUNT RECEIVED	AMOUNT NOT RECEIVED	LATE FEES	COMMENTS
JANUARY					
FEBRUARY					
MARCH					
APRIL					
MAY					
JUNE					
JULY					
AUGUST					
SEPTEMBER					
OCTOBER					
NOVEMBER					
DECEMBER					
TOTALS					

NOTES

RENTAL LEDGER BOOK

YEAR	
TENANT	
ADDRESS	
AMOUNT OF MONTHLY RENT	DATE DUE

MONTH	DAY RENT RECEIVED	AMOUNT RECEIVED	AMOUNT NOT RECEIVED	LATE FEES	COMMENTS
JANUARY					
FEBRUARY					
MARCH					
APRIL					
MAY					
JUNE					
JULY					
AUGUST					
SEPTEMBER					
OCTOBER					
NOVEMBER					
DECEMBER					
TOTALS					

NOTES

RENTAL LEDGER BOOK

YEAR	
TENANT	
ADDRESS	
AMOUNT OF MONTHLY RENT		DATE DUE	

MONTH	DAY RENT RECEIVED	AMOUNT RECEIVED	AMOUNT NOT RECEIVED	LATE FEES	COMMENTS
JANUARY					
FEBRUARY					
MARCH					
APRIL					
MAY					
JUNE					
JULY					
AUGUST					
SEPTEMBER					
OCTOBER					
NOVEMBER					
DECEMBER					
TOTALS					

NOTES

RENTAL LEDGER BOOK

YEAR	
TENANT	
ADDRESS	

AMOUNT OF MONTHLY RENT		DATE DUE	

MONTH	DAY RENT RECEIVED	AMOUNT RECEIVED	AMOUNT NOT RECEIVED	LATE FEES	COMMENTS
JANUARY					
FEBRUARY					
MARCH					
APRIL					
MAY					
JUNE					
JULY					
AUGUST					
SEPTEMBER					
OCTOBER					
NOVEMBER					
DECEMBER					
TOTALS					

NOTES

RENTAL LEDGER BOOK

YEAR	
TENANT	
ADDRESS	

AMOUNT OF MONTHLY RENT		DATE DUE	

MONTH	DAY RENT RECEIVED	AMOUNT RECEIVED	AMOUNT NOT RECEIVED	LATE FEES	COMMENTS
JANUARY					
FEBRUARY					
MARCH					
APRIL					
MAY					
JUNE					
JULY					
AUGUST					
SEPTEMBER					
OCTOBER					
NOVEMBER					
DECEMBER					
TOTALS					

NOTES

RENTAL LEDGER BOOK

YEAR	
TENANT	
ADDRESS	
AMOUNT OF MONTHLY RENT	DATE DUE

MONTH	DAY RENT RECEIVED	AMOUNT RECEIVED	AMOUNT NOT RECEIVED	LATE FEES	COMMENTS
JANUARY					
FEBRUARY					
MARCH					
APRIL					
MAY					
JUNE					
JULY					
AUGUST					
SEPTEMBER					
OCTOBER					
NOVEMBER					
DECEMBER					
TOTALS					

NOTES

RENTAL LEDGER BOOK

YEAR	
TENANT	
ADDRESS	
AMOUNT OF MONTHLY RENT	DATE DUE

MONTH	DAY RENT RECEIVED	AMOUNT RECEIVED	AMOUNT NOT RECEIVED	LATE FEES	COMMENTS
JANUARY					
FEBRUARY					
MARCH					
APRIL					
MAY					
JUNE					
JULY					
AUGUST					
SEPTEMBER					
OCTOBER					
NOVEMBER					
DECEMBER					
TOTALS					

NOTES

RENTAL LEDGER BOOK

YEAR	
TENANT	
ADDRESS	
AMOUNT OF MONTHLY RENT	DATE DUE

MONTH	DAY RENT RECEIVED	AMOUNT RECEIVED	AMOUNT NOT RECEIVED	LATE FEES	COMMENTS
JANUARY					
FEBRUARY					
MARCH					
APRIL					
MAY					
JUNE					
JULY					
AUGUST					
SEPTEMBER					
OCTOBER					
NOVEMBER					
DECEMBER					
TOTALS					

NOTES

RENTAL LEDGER BOOK

YEAR	
TENANT	
ADDRESS	
AMOUNT OF MONTHLY RENT	DATE DUE

MONTH	DAY RENT RECEIVED	AMOUNT RECEIVED	AMOUNT NOT RECEIVED	LATE FEES	COMMENTS
JANUARY					
FEBRUARY					
MARCH					
APRIL					
MAY					
JUNE					
JULY					
AUGUST					
SEPTEMBER					
OCTOBER					
NOVEMBER					
DECEMBER					
TOTALS					

NOTES

RENTAL LEDGER BOOK

YEAR	
TENANT	
ADDRESS	
AMOUNT OF MONTHLY RENT	DATE DUE

MONTH	DAY RENT RECEIVED	AMOUNT RECEIVED	AMOUNT NOT RECEIVED	LATE FEES	COMMENTS
JANUARY					
FEBRUARY					
MARCH					
APRIL					
MAY					
JUNE					
JULY					
AUGUST					
SEPTEMBER					
OCTOBER					
NOVEMBER					
DECEMBER					
TOTALS					

NOTES

RENTAL LEDGER BOOK

YEAR	
TENANT	
ADDRESS	
AMOUNT OF MONTHLY RENT	DATE DUE

MONTH	DAY RENT RECEIVED	AMOUNT RECEIVED	AMOUNT NOT RECEIVED	LATE FEES	COMMENTS
JANUARY					
FEBRUARY					
MARCH					
APRIL					
MAY					
JUNE					
JULY					
AUGUST					
SEPTEMBER					
OCTOBER					
NOVEMBER					
DECEMBER					
TOTALS					

NOTES

RENTAL LEDGER BOOK

YEAR	
TENANT	
ADDRESS	
AMOUNT OF MONTHLY RENT		DATE DUE	

MONTH	DAY RENT RECEIVED	AMOUNT RECEIVED	AMOUNT NOT RECEIVED	LATE FEES	COMMENTS
JANUARY					
FEBRUARY					
MARCH					
APRIL					
MAY					
JUNE					
JULY					
AUGUST					
SEPTEMBER					
OCTOBER					
NOVEMBER					
DECEMBER					
TOTALS					

NOTES

RENTAL LEDGER BOOK

YEAR	
TENANT	
ADDRESS	
AMOUNT OF MONTHLY RENT	DATE DUE

MONTH	DAY RENT RECEIVED	AMOUNT RECEIVED	AMOUNT NOT RECEIVED	LATE FEES	COMMENTS
JANUARY					
FEBRUARY					
MARCH					
APRIL					
MAY					
JUNE					
JULY					
AUGUST					
SEPTEMBER					
OCTOBER					
NOVEMBER					
DECEMBER					
TOTALS					

NOTES

RENTAL LEDGER BOOK

YEAR	
TENANT	
ADDRESS	
AMOUNT OF MONTHLY RENT	

DATE DUE	

MONTH	DAY RENT RECEIVED	AMOUNT RECEIVED	AMOUNT NOT RECEIVED	LATE FEES	COMMENTS
JANUARY					
FEBRUARY					
MARCH					
APRIL					
MAY					
JUNE					
JULY					
AUGUST					
SEPTEMBER					
OCTOBER					
NOVEMBER					
DECEMBER					
TOTALS					

NOTES

RENTAL LEDGER BOOK

YEAR	
TENANT	
ADDRESS	
AMOUNT OF MONTHLY RENT	DATE DUE

MONTH	DAY RENT RECEIVED	AMOUNT RECEIVED	AMOUNT NOT RECEIVED	LATE FEES	COMMENTS
JANUARY					
FEBRUARY					
MARCH					
APRIL					
MAY					
JUNE					
JULY					
AUGUST					
SEPTEMBER					
OCTOBER					
NOVEMBER					
DECEMBER					
TOTALS					

NOTES

RENTAL LEDGER BOOK

YEAR	
TENANT	
ADDRESS	
AMOUNT OF MONTHLY RENT	DATE DUE

MONTH	DAY RENT RECEIVED	AMOUNT RECEIVED	AMOUNT NOT RECEIVED	LATE FEES	COMMENTS
JANUARY					
FEBRUARY					
MARCH					
APRIL					
MAY					
JUNE					
JULY					
AUGUST					
SEPTEMBER					
OCTOBER					
NOVEMBER					
DECEMBER					
TOTALS					

NOTES

RENTAL LEDGER BOOK

YEAR	
TENANT	
ADDRESS	
AMOUNT OF MONTHLY RENT	DATE DUE

MONTH	DAY RENT RECEIVED	AMOUNT RECEIVED	AMOUNT NOT RECEIVED	LATE FEES	COMMENTS
JANUARY					
FEBRUARY					
MARCH					
APRIL					
MAY					
JUNE					
JULY					
AUGUST					
SEPTEMBER					
OCTOBER					
NOVEMBER					
DECEMBER					
TOTALS					

NOTES

RENTAL LEDGER BOOK

YEAR	
TENANT	
ADDRESS	
AMOUNT OF MONTHLY RENT	DATE DUE

MONTH	DAY RENT RECEIVED	AMOUNT RECEIVED	AMOUNT NOT RECEIVED	LATE FEES	COMMENTS
JANUARY					
FEBRUARY					
MARCH					
APRIL					
MAY					
JUNE					
JULY					
AUGUST					
SEPTEMBER					
OCTOBER					
NOVEMBER					
DECEMBER					
TOTALS					

NOTES

RENTAL LEDGER BOOK

YEAR	
TENANT	
ADDRESS	
AMOUNT OF MONTHLY RENT	DATE DUE

MONTH	DAY RENT RECEIVED	AMOUNT RECEIVED	AMOUNT NOT RECEIVED	LATE FEES	COMMENTS
JANUARY					
FEBRUARY					
MARCH					
APRIL					
MAY					
JUNE					
JULY					
AUGUST					
SEPTEMBER					
OCTOBER					
NOVEMBER					
DECEMBER					
TOTALS					

NOTES

RENTAL LEDGER BOOK

YEAR	
TENANT	
ADDRESS	
AMOUNT OF MONTHLY RENT	DATE DUE

MONTH	DAY RENT RECEIVED	AMOUNT RECEIVED	AMOUNT NOT RECEIVED	LATE FEES	COMMENTS
JANUARY					
FEBRUARY					
MARCH					
APRIL					
MAY					
JUNE					
JULY					
AUGUST					
SEPTEMBER					
OCTOBER					
NOVEMBER					
DECEMBER					
TOTALS					

NOTES

RENTAL LEDGER BOOK

YEAR	
TENANT	
ADDRESS	
AMOUNT OF MONTHLY RENT	DATE DUE

MONTH	DAY RENT RECEIVED	AMOUNT RECEIVED	AMOUNT NOT RECEIVED	LATE FEES	COMMENTS
JANUARY					
FEBRUARY					
MARCH					
APRIL					
MAY					
JUNE					
JULY					
AUGUST					
SEPTEMBER					
OCTOBER					
NOVEMBER					
DECEMBER					
TOTALS					

NOTES

RENTAL LEDGER BOOK

YEAR	
TENANT	
ADDRESS	
AMOUNT OF MONTHLY RENT	DATE DUE

MONTH	DAY RENT RECEIVED	AMOUNT RECEIVED	AMOUNT NOT RECEIVED	LATE FEES	COMMENTS
JANUARY					
FEBRUARY					
MARCH					
APRIL					
MAY					
JUNE					
JULY					
AUGUST					
SEPTEMBER					
OCTOBER					
NOVEMBER					
DECEMBER					
TOTALS					

NOTES

RENTAL LEDGER BOOK

YEAR	
TENANT	
ADDRESS	
AMOUNT OF MONTHLY RENT	DATE DUE

MONTH	DAY RENT RECEIVED	AMOUNT RECEIVED	AMOUNT NOT RECEIVED	LATE FEES	COMMENTS
JANUARY					
FEBRUARY					
MARCH					
APRIL					
MAY					
JUNE					
JULY					
AUGUST					
SEPTEMBER					
OCTOBER					
NOVEMBER					
DECEMBER					
TOTALS					

NOTES

RENTAL LEDGER BOOK

YEAR	
TENANT	
ADDRESS	
AMOUNT OF MONTHLY RENT	DATE DUE

MONTH	DAY RENT RECEIVED	AMOUNT RECEIVED	AMOUNT NOT RECEIVED	LATE FEES	COMMENTS
JANUARY					
FEBRUARY					
MARCH					
APRIL					
MAY					
JUNE					
JULY					
AUGUST					
SEPTEMBER					
OCTOBER					
NOVEMBER					
DECEMBER					
TOTALS					

NOTES

RENTAL LEDGER BOOK

YEAR	
TENANT	
ADDRESS	
AMOUNT OF MONTHLY RENT	DATE DUE

MONTH	DAY RENT RECEIVED	AMOUNT RECEIVED	AMOUNT NOT RECEIVED	LATE FEES	COMMENTS
JANUARY					
FEBRUARY					
MARCH					
APRIL					
MAY					
JUNE					
JULY					
AUGUST					
SEPTEMBER					
OCTOBER					
NOVEMBER					
DECEMBER					
TOTALS					

NOTES

RENTAL LEDGER BOOK

YEAR	
TENANT	
ADDRESS	
AMOUNT OF MONTHLY RENT	DATE DUE

MONTH	DAY RENT RECEIVED	AMOUNT RECEIVED	AMOUNT NOT RECEIVED	LATE FEES	COMMENTS
JANUARY					
FEBRUARY					
MARCH					
APRIL					
MAY					
JUNE					
JULY					
AUGUST					
SEPTEMBER					
OCTOBER					
NOVEMBER					
DECEMBER					
TOTALS					

NOTES

RENTAL LEDGER BOOK

YEAR	
TENANT	
ADDRESS	
AMOUNT OF MONTHLY RENT	DATE DUE

MONTH	DAY RENT RECEIVED	AMOUNT RECEIVED	AMOUNT NOT RECEIVED	LATE FEES	COMMENTS
JANUARY					
FEBRUARY					
MARCH					
APRIL					
MAY					
JUNE					
JULY					
AUGUST					
SEPTEMBER					
OCTOBER					
NOVEMBER					
DECEMBER					
TOTALS					

NOTES

RENTAL LEDGER BOOK

YEAR	
TENANT	
ADDRESS	
AMOUNT OF MONTHLY RENT		DATE DUE	

MONTH	DAY RENT RECEIVED	AMOUNT RECEIVED	AMOUNT NOT RECEIVED	LATE FEES	COMMENTS
JANUARY					
FEBRUARY					
MARCH					
APRIL					
MAY					
JUNE					
JULY					
AUGUST					
SEPTEMBER					
OCTOBER					
NOVEMBER					
DECEMBER					
TOTALS					

NOTES

RENTAL LEDGER BOOK

YEAR	
TENANT	
ADDRESS	
AMOUNT OF MONTHLY RENT	DATE DUE

MONTH	DAY RENT RECEIVED	AMOUNT RECEIVED	AMOUNT NOT RECEIVED	LATE FEES	COMMENTS
JANUARY					
FEBRUARY					
MARCH					
APRIL					
MAY					
JUNE					
JULY					
AUGUST					
SEPTEMBER					
OCTOBER					
NOVEMBER					
DECEMBER					
TOTALS					

NOTES

RENTAL LEDGER BOOK

YEAR	
TENANT	
ADDRESS	
AMOUNT OF MONTHLY RENT	DATE DUE

MONTH	DAY RENT RECEIVED	AMOUNT RECEIVED	AMOUNT NOT RECEIVED	LATE FEES	COMMENTS
JANUARY					
FEBRUARY					
MARCH					
APRIL					
MAY					
JUNE					
JULY					
AUGUST					
SEPTEMBER					
OCTOBER					
NOVEMBER					
DECEMBER					
TOTALS					

NOTES

RENTAL LEDGER BOOK

YEAR	
TENANT	
ADDRESS	
AMOUNT OF MONTHLY RENT	DATE DUE

MONTH	DAY RENT RECEIVED	AMOUNT RECEIVED	AMOUNT NOT RECEIVED	LATE FEES	COMMENTS
JANUARY					
FEBRUARY					
MARCH					
APRIL					
MAY					
JUNE					
JULY					
AUGUST					
SEPTEMBER					
OCTOBER					
NOVEMBER					
DECEMBER					
TOTALS					

NOTES

RENTAL LEDGER BOOK

YEAR	
TENANT	
ADDRESS	
AMOUNT OF MONTHLY RENT	DATE DUE

MONTH	DAY RENT RECEIVED	AMOUNT RECEIVED	AMOUNT NOT RECEIVED	LATE FEES	COMMENTS
JANUARY					
FEBRUARY					
MARCH					
APRIL					
MAY					
JUNE					
JULY					
AUGUST					
SEPTEMBER					
OCTOBER					
NOVEMBER					
DECEMBER					
TOTALS					

NOTES

RENTAL LEDGER BOOK

YEAR	
TENANT	
ADDRESS	
AMOUNT OF MONTHLY RENT	DATE DUE

MONTH	DAY RENT RECEIVED	AMOUNT RECEIVED	AMOUNT NOT RECEIVED	LATE FEES	COMMENTS
JANUARY					
FEBRUARY					
MARCH					
APRIL					
MAY					
JUNE					
JULY					
AUGUST					
SEPTEMBER					
OCTOBER					
NOVEMBER					
DECEMBER					
TOTALS					

NOTES

RENTAL LEDGER BOOK

YEAR	
TENANT	
ADDRESS	
AMOUNT OF MONTHLY RENT	DATE DUE

MONTH	DAY RENT RECEIVED	AMOUNT RECEIVED	AMOUNT NOT RECEIVED	LATE FEES	COMMENTS
JANUARY					
FEBRUARY					
MARCH					
APRIL					
MAY					
JUNE					
JULY					
AUGUST					
SEPTEMBER					
OCTOBER					
NOVEMBER					
DECEMBER					
TOTALS					

NOTES

RENTAL LEDGER BOOK

YEAR	
TENANT	
ADDRESS	
AMOUNT OF MONTHLY RENT	DATE DUE

MONTH	DAY RENT RECEIVED	AMOUNT RECEIVED	AMOUNT NOT RECEIVED	LATE FEES	COMMENTS
JANUARY					
FEBRUARY					
MARCH					
APRIL					
MAY					
JUNE					
JULY					
AUGUST					
SEPTEMBER					
OCTOBER					
NOVEMBER					
DECEMBER					
TOTALS					

NOTES

RENTAL LEDGER BOOK

YEAR	
TENANT	
ADDRESS	
AMOUNT OF MONTHLY RENT	DATE DUE

MONTH	DAY RENT RECEIVED	AMOUNT RECEIVED	AMOUNT NOT RECEIVED	LATE FEES	COMMENTS
JANUARY					
FEBRUARY					
MARCH					
APRIL					
MAY					
JUNE					
JULY					
AUGUST					
SEPTEMBER					
OCTOBER					
NOVEMBER					
DECEMBER					
TOTALS					

NOTES

RENTAL LEDGER BOOK

YEAR	
TENANT	
ADDRESS	
AMOUNT OF MONTHLY RENT	DATE DUE

MONTH	DAY RENT RECEIVED	AMOUNT RECEIVED	AMOUNT NOT RECEIVED	LATE FEES	COMMENTS
JANUARY					
FEBRUARY					
MARCH					
APRIL					
MAY					
JUNE					
JULY					
AUGUST					
SEPTEMBER					
OCTOBER					
NOVEMBER					
DECEMBER					
TOTALS					

NOTES

RENTAL LEDGER BOOK

YEAR	
TENANT	
ADDRESS	
AMOUNT OF MONTHLY RENT	DATE DUE

MONTH	DAY RENT RECEIVED	AMOUNT RECEIVED	AMOUNT NOT RECEIVED	LATE FEES	COMMENTS
JANUARY					
FEBRUARY					
MARCH					
APRIL					
MAY					
JUNE					
JULY					
AUGUST					
SEPTEMBER					
OCTOBER					
NOVEMBER					
DECEMBER					
TOTALS					

NOTES

RENTAL LEDGER BOOK

YEAR	
TENANT	
ADDRESS	
AMOUNT OF MONTHLY RENT	DATE DUE

MONTH	DAY RENT RECEIVED	AMOUNT RECEIVED	AMOUNT NOT RECEIVED	LATE FEES	COMMENTS
JANUARY					
FEBRUARY					
MARCH					
APRIL					
MAY					
JUNE					
JULY					
AUGUST					
SEPTEMBER					
OCTOBER					
NOVEMBER					
DECEMBER					
TOTALS					

NOTES

RENTAL LEDGER BOOK

YEAR	
TENANT	
ADDRESS	
AMOUNT OF MONTHLY RENT	DATE DUE

MONTH	DAY RENT RECEIVED	AMOUNT RECEIVED	AMOUNT NOT RECEIVED	LATE FEES	COMMENTS
JANUARY					
FEBRUARY					
MARCH					
APRIL					
MAY					
JUNE					
JULY					
AUGUST					
SEPTEMBER					
OCTOBER					
NOVEMBER					
DECEMBER					
TOTALS					

NOTES

RENTAL LEDGER BOOK

YEAR	
TENANT	
ADDRESS	
AMOUNT OF MONTHLY RENT	DATE DUE

MONTH	DAY RENT RECEIVED	AMOUNT RECEIVED	AMOUNT NOT RECEIVED	LATE FEES	COMMENTS
JANUARY					
FEBRUARY					
MARCH					
APRIL					
MAY					
JUNE					
JULY					
AUGUST					
SEPTEMBER					
OCTOBER					
NOVEMBER					
DECEMBER					
TOTALS					

NOTES

RENTAL LEDGER BOOK

YEAR	
TENANT	
ADDRESS	
AMOUNT OF MONTHLY RENT	DATE DUE

MONTH	DAY RENT RECEIVED	AMOUNT RECEIVED	AMOUNT NOT RECEIVED	LATE FEES	COMMENTS
JANUARY					
FEBRUARY					
MARCH					
APRIL					
MAY					
JUNE					
JULY					
AUGUST					
SEPTEMBER					
OCTOBER					
NOVEMBER					
DECEMBER					
TOTALS					

NOTES

RENTAL LEDGER BOOK

YEAR	
TENANT	
ADDRESS	
AMOUNT OF MONTHLY RENT		DATE DUE	

MONTH	DAY RENT RECEIVED	AMOUNT RECEIVED	AMOUNT NOT RECEIVED	LATE FEES	COMMENTS
JANUARY					
FEBRUARY					
MARCH					
APRIL					
MAY					
JUNE					
JULY					
AUGUST					
SEPTEMBER					
OCTOBER					
NOVEMBER					
DECEMBER					
TOTALS					

NOTES

RENTAL LEDGER BOOK

YEAR	
TENANT	
ADDRESS	
AMOUNT OF MONTHLY RENT	DATE DUE

MONTH	DAY RENT RECEIVED	AMOUNT RECEIVED	AMOUNT NOT RECEIVED	LATE FEES	COMMENTS
JANUARY					
FEBRUARY					
MARCH					
APRIL					
MAY					
JUNE					
JULY					
AUGUST					
SEPTEMBER					
OCTOBER					
NOVEMBER					
DECEMBER					
TOTALS					

NOTES

RENTAL LEDGER BOOK

YEAR	
TENANT	
ADDRESS	
AMOUNT OF MONTHLY RENT	DATE DUE

MONTH	DAY RENT RECEIVED	AMOUNT RECEIVED	AMOUNT NOT RECEIVED	LATE FEES	COMMENTS
JANUARY					
FEBRUARY					
MARCH					
APRIL					
MAY					
JUNE					
JULY					
AUGUST					
SEPTEMBER					
OCTOBER					
NOVEMBER					
DECEMBER					
TOTALS					

NOTES

RENTAL LEDGER BOOK

YEAR	
TENANT	
ADDRESS	
AMOUNT OF MONTHLY RENT	DATE DUE

MONTH	DAY RENT RECEIVED	AMOUNT RECEIVED	AMOUNT NOT RECEIVED	LATE FEES	COMMENTS
JANUARY					
FEBRUARY					
MARCH					
APRIL					
MAY					
JUNE					
JULY					
AUGUST					
SEPTEMBER					
OCTOBER					
NOVEMBER					
DECEMBER					
TOTALS					

NOTES

RENTAL LEDGER BOOK

YEAR	
TENANT	
ADDRESS	
AMOUNT OF MONTHLY RENT	DATE DUE

MONTH	DAY RENT RECEIVED	AMOUNT RECEIVED	AMOUNT NOT RECEIVED	LATE FEES	COMMENTS
JANUARY					
FEBRUARY					
MARCH					
APRIL					
MAY					
JUNE					
JULY					
AUGUST					
SEPTEMBER					
OCTOBER					
NOVEMBER					
DECEMBER					
TOTALS					

NOTES

RENTAL LEDGER BOOK

YEAR	
TENANT	
ADDRESS	
AMOUNT OF MONTHLY RENT		DATE DUE	

MONTH	DAY RENT RECEIVED	AMOUNT RECEIVED	AMOUNT NOT RECEIVED	LATE FEES	COMMENTS
JANUARY					
FEBRUARY					
MARCH					
APRIL					
MAY					
JUNE					
JULY					
AUGUST					
SEPTEMBER					
OCTOBER					
NOVEMBER					
DECEMBER					
TOTALS					

NOTES

RENTAL LEDGER BOOK

YEAR	
TENANT	
ADDRESS	
AMOUNT OF MONTHLY RENT	DATE DUE

MONTH	DAY RENT RECEIVED	AMOUNT RECEIVED	AMOUNT NOT RECEIVED	LATE FEES	COMMENTS
JANUARY					
FEBRUARY					
MARCH					
APRIL					
MAY					
JUNE					
JULY					
AUGUST					
SEPTEMBER					
OCTOBER					
NOVEMBER					
DECEMBER					
TOTALS					

NOTES

RENTAL LEDGER BOOK

YEAR	
TENANT	
ADDRESS	
AMOUNT OF MONTHLY RENT	DATE DUE

MONTH	DAY RENT RECEIVED	AMOUNT RECEIVED	AMOUNT NOT RECEIVED	LATE FEES	COMMENTS
JANUARY					
FEBRUARY					
MARCH					
APRIL					
MAY					
JUNE					
JULY					
AUGUST					
SEPTEMBER					
OCTOBER					
NOVEMBER					
DECEMBER					
TOTALS					

NOTES

RENTAL LEDGER BOOK

YEAR	
TENANT	
ADDRESS	
AMOUNT OF MONTHLY RENT	DATE DUE

MONTH	DAY RENT RECEIVED	AMOUNT RECEIVED	AMOUNT NOT RECEIVED	LATE FEES	COMMENTS
JANUARY					
FEBRUARY					
MARCH					
APRIL					
MAY					
JUNE					
JULY					
AUGUST					
SEPTEMBER					
OCTOBER					
NOVEMBER					
DECEMBER					
TOTALS					

NOTES

RENTAL LEDGER BOOK

YEAR	
TENANT	
ADDRESS	
AMOUNT OF MONTHLY RENT	DATE DUE

MONTH	DAY RENT RECEIVED	AMOUNT RECEIVED	AMOUNT NOT RECEIVED	LATE FEES	COMMENTS
JANUARY					
FEBRUARY					
MARCH					
APRIL					
MAY					
JUNE					
JULY					
AUGUST					
SEPTEMBER					
OCTOBER					
NOVEMBER					
DECEMBER					
TOTALS					

NOTES

RENTAL LEDGER BOOK

YEAR	
TENANT	
ADDRESS	
AMOUNT OF MONTHLY RENT	DATE DUE

MONTH	DAY RENT RECEIVED	AMOUNT RECEIVED	AMOUNT NOT RECEIVED	LATE FEES	COMMENTS
JANUARY					
FEBRUARY					
MARCH					
APRIL					
MAY					
JUNE					
JULY					
AUGUST					
SEPTEMBER					
OCTOBER					
NOVEMBER					
DECEMBER					
TOTALS					

NOTES

RENTAL LEDGER BOOK

YEAR	
TENANT	
ADDRESS	
AMOUNT OF MONTHLY RENT	DATE DUE

MONTH	DAY RENT RECEIVED	AMOUNT RECEIVED	AMOUNT NOT RECEIVED	LATE FEES	COMMENTS
JANUARY					
FEBRUARY					
MARCH					
APRIL					
MAY					
JUNE					
JULY					
AUGUST					
SEPTEMBER					
OCTOBER					
NOVEMBER					
DECEMBER					
TOTALS					

NOTES

RENTAL LEDGER BOOK

YEAR	
TENANT	
ADDRESS	
AMOUNT OF MONTHLY RENT	DATE DUE

MONTH	DAY RENT RECEIVED	AMOUNT RECEIVED	AMOUNT NOT RECEIVED	LATE FEES	COMMENTS
JANUARY					
FEBRUARY					
MARCH					
APRIL					
MAY					
JUNE					
JULY					
AUGUST					
SEPTEMBER					
OCTOBER					
NOVEMBER					
DECEMBER					
TOTALS					

NOTES

RENTAL LEDGER BOOK

YEAR	
TENANT	
ADDRESS	
AMOUNT OF MONTHLY RENT	DATE DUE

MONTH	DAY RENT RECEIVED	AMOUNT RECEIVED	AMOUNT NOT RECEIVED	LATE FEES	COMMENTS
JANUARY					
FEBRUARY					
MARCH					
APRIL					
MAY					
JUNE					
JULY					
AUGUST					
SEPTEMBER					
OCTOBER					
NOVEMBER					
DECEMBER					
TOTALS					

NOTES

RENTAL LEDGER BOOK

YEAR	
TENANT	
ADDRESS	
AMOUNT OF MONTHLY RENT	DATE DUE

MONTH	DAY RENT RECEIVED	AMOUNT RECEIVED	AMOUNT NOT RECEIVED	LATE FEES	COMMENTS
JANUARY					
FEBRUARY					
MARCH					
APRIL					
MAY					
JUNE					
JULY					
AUGUST					
SEPTEMBER					
OCTOBER					
NOVEMBER					
DECEMBER					
TOTALS					

NOTES

RENTAL LEDGER BOOK

YEAR	
TENANT	
ADDRESS	
AMOUNT OF MONTHLY RENT	DATE DUE

MONTH	DAY RENT RECEIVED	AMOUNT RECEIVED	AMOUNT NOT RECEIVED	LATE FEES	COMMENTS
JANUARY					
FEBRUARY					
MARCH					
APRIL					
MAY					
JUNE					
JULY					
AUGUST					
SEPTEMBER					
OCTOBER					
NOVEMBER					
DECEMBER					
TOTALS					

NOTES

RENTAL LEDGER BOOK

YEAR	
TENANT	
ADDRESS	
AMOUNT OF MONTHLY RENT	DATE DUE

MONTH	DAY RENT RECEIVED	AMOUNT RECEIVED	AMOUNT NOT RECEIVED	LATE FEES	COMMENTS
JANUARY					
FEBRUARY					
MARCH					
APRIL					
MAY					
JUNE					
JULY					
AUGUST					
SEPTEMBER					
OCTOBER					
NOVEMBER					
DECEMBER					
TOTALS					

NOTES

RENTAL LEDGER BOOK

YEAR	
TENANT	
ADDRESS	
AMOUNT OF MONTHLY RENT	DATE DUE

MONTH	DAY RENT RECEIVED	AMOUNT RECEIVED	AMOUNT NOT RECEIVED	LATE FEES	COMMENTS
JANUARY					
FEBRUARY					
MARCH					
APRIL					
MAY					
JUNE					
JULY					
AUGUST					
SEPTEMBER					
OCTOBER					
NOVEMBER					
DECEMBER					
TOTALS					

NOTES

RENTAL LEDGER BOOK

YEAR	
TENANT	
ADDRESS	
AMOUNT OF MONTHLY RENT	DATE DUE

MONTH	DAY RENT RECEIVED	AMOUNT RECEIVED	AMOUNT NOT RECEIVED	LATE FEES	COMMENTS
JANUARY					
FEBRUARY					
MARCH					
APRIL					
MAY					
JUNE					
JULY					
AUGUST					
SEPTEMBER					
OCTOBER					
NOVEMBER					
DECEMBER					
TOTALS					

NOTES

RENTAL LEDGER BOOK

YEAR	
TENANT	
ADDRESS	
AMOUNT OF MONTHLY RENT	DATE DUE

MONTH	DAY RENT RECEIVED	AMOUNT RECEIVED	AMOUNT NOT RECEIVED	LATE FEES	COMMENTS
JANUARY					
FEBRUARY					
MARCH					
APRIL					
MAY					
JUNE					
JULY					
AUGUST					
SEPTEMBER					
OCTOBER					
NOVEMBER					
DECEMBER					
TOTALS					

NOTES

RENTAL LEDGER BOOK

YEAR	
TENANT	
ADDRESS	
AMOUNT OF MONTHLY RENT	DATE DUE

MONTH	DAY RENT RECEIVED	AMOUNT RECEIVED	AMOUNT NOT RECEIVED	LATE FEES	COMMENTS
JANUARY					
FEBRUARY					
MARCH					
APRIL					
MAY					
JUNE					
JULY					
AUGUST					
SEPTEMBER					
OCTOBER					
NOVEMBER					
DECEMBER					
TOTALS					

NOTES

RENTAL LEDGER BOOK

YEAR	
TENANT	
ADDRESS	
AMOUNT OF MONTHLY RENT	DATE DUE

MONTH	DAY RENT RECEIVED	AMOUNT RECEIVED	AMOUNT NOT RECEIVED	LATE FEES	COMMENTS
JANUARY					
FEBRUARY					
MARCH					
APRIL					
MAY					
JUNE					
JULY					
AUGUST					
SEPTEMBER					
OCTOBER					
NOVEMBER					
DECEMBER					
TOTALS					

NOTES

RENTAL LEDGER BOOK

YEAR	
TENANT	
ADDRESS	
AMOUNT OF MONTHLY RENT	DATE DUE

MONTH	DAY RENT RECEIVED	AMOUNT RECEIVED	AMOUNT NOT RECEIVED	LATE FEES	COMMENTS
JANUARY					
FEBRUARY					
MARCH					
APRIL					
MAY					
JUNE					
JULY					
AUGUST					
SEPTEMBER					
OCTOBER					
NOVEMBER					
DECEMBER					
TOTALS					

NOTES

RENTAL LEDGER BOOK

YEAR	
TENANT	
ADDRESS	
AMOUNT OF MONTHLY RENT	DATE DUE

MONTH	DAY RENT RECEIVED	AMOUNT RECEIVED	AMOUNT NOT RECEIVED	LATE FEES	COMMENTS
JANUARY					
FEBRUARY					
MARCH					
APRIL					
MAY					
JUNE					
JULY					
AUGUST					
SEPTEMBER					
OCTOBER					
NOVEMBER					
DECEMBER					
TOTALS					

NOTES

RENTAL LEDGER BOOK

YEAR	
TENANT	
ADDRESS	
AMOUNT OF MONTHLY RENT	DATE DUE

MONTH	DAY RENT RECEIVED	AMOUNT RECEIVED	AMOUNT NOT RECEIVED	LATE FEES	COMMENTS
JANUARY					
FEBRUARY					
MARCH					
APRIL					
MAY					
JUNE					
JULY					
AUGUST					
SEPTEMBER					
OCTOBER					
NOVEMBER					
DECEMBER					
TOTALS					

NOTES

RENTAL LEDGER BOOK

YEAR	
TENANT	
ADDRESS	
AMOUNT OF MONTHLY RENT	DATE DUE

MONTH	DAY RENT RECEIVED	AMOUNT RECEIVED	AMOUNT NOT RECEIVED	LATE FEES	COMMENTS
JANUARY					
FEBRUARY					
MARCH					
APRIL					
MAY					
JUNE					
JULY					
AUGUST					
SEPTEMBER					
OCTOBER					
NOVEMBER					
DECEMBER					
TOTALS					

NOTES

RENTAL LEDGER BOOK

YEAR	
TENANT	
ADDRESS	
AMOUNT OF MONTHLY RENT	DATE DUE

MONTH	DAY RENT RECEIVED	AMOUNT RECEIVED	AMOUNT NOT RECEIVED	LATE FEES	COMMENTS
JANUARY					
FEBRUARY					
MARCH					
APRIL					
MAY					
JUNE					
JULY					
AUGUST					
SEPTEMBER					
OCTOBER					
NOVEMBER					
DECEMBER					
TOTALS					

NOTES

RENTAL LEDGER BOOK

YEAR	
TENANT	
ADDRESS	
AMOUNT OF MONTHLY RENT	DATE DUE

MONTH	DAY RENT RECEIVED	AMOUNT RECEIVED	AMOUNT NOT RECEIVED	LATE FEES	COMMENTS
JANUARY					
FEBRUARY					
MARCH					
APRIL					
MAY					
JUNE					
JULY					
AUGUST					
SEPTEMBER					
OCTOBER					
NOVEMBER					
DECEMBER					
TOTALS					

NOTES

RENTAL LEDGER BOOK

YEAR	
TENANT	
ADDRESS	
AMOUNT OF MONTHLY RENT	DATE DUE

MONTH	DAY RENT RECEIVED	AMOUNT RECEIVED	AMOUNT NOT RECEIVED	LATE FEES	COMMENTS
JANUARY					
FEBRUARY					
MARCH					
APRIL					
MAY					
JUNE					
JULY					
AUGUST					
SEPTEMBER					
OCTOBER					
NOVEMBER					
DECEMBER					
TOTALS					

NOTES

RENTAL LEDGER BOOK

YEAR	
TENANT	
ADDRESS	
AMOUNT OF MONTHLY RENT	DATE DUE

MONTH	DAY RENT RECEIVED	AMOUNT RECEIVED	AMOUNT NOT RECEIVED	LATE FEES	COMMENTS
JANUARY					
FEBRUARY					
MARCH					
APRIL					
MAY					
JUNE					
JULY					
AUGUST					
SEPTEMBER					
OCTOBER					
NOVEMBER					
DECEMBER					
TOTALS					

NOTES

RENTAL LEDGER BOOK

YEAR	
TENANT	
ADDRESS	
AMOUNT OF MONTHLY RENT	DATE DUE

MONTH	DAY RENT RECEIVED	AMOUNT RECEIVED	AMOUNT NOT RECEIVED	LATE FEES	COMMENTS
JANUARY					
FEBRUARY					
MARCH					
APRIL					
MAY					
JUNE					
JULY					
AUGUST					
SEPTEMBER					
OCTOBER					
NOVEMBER					
DECEMBER					
TOTALS					

NOTES

RENTAL LEDGER BOOK

YEAR	
TENANT	
ADDRESS	
AMOUNT OF MONTHLY RENT	DATE DUE

MONTH	DAY RENT RECEIVED	AMOUNT RECEIVED	AMOUNT NOT RECEIVED	LATE FEES	COMMENTS
JANUARY					
FEBRUARY					
MARCH					
APRIL					
MAY					
JUNE					
JULY					
AUGUST					
SEPTEMBER					
OCTOBER					
NOVEMBER					
DECEMBER					
TOTALS					

NOTES

RENTAL LEDGER BOOK

YEAR	
TENANT	
ADDRESS	
AMOUNT OF MONTHLY RENT	DATE DUE

MONTH	DAY RENT RECEIVED	AMOUNT RECEIVED	AMOUNT NOT RECEIVED	LATE FEES	COMMENTS
JANUARY					
FEBRUARY					
MARCH					
APRIL					
MAY					
JUNE					
JULY					
AUGUST					
SEPTEMBER					
OCTOBER					
NOVEMBER					
DECEMBER					
TOTALS					

NOTES

RENTAL LEDGER BOOK

YEAR	
TENANT	
ADDRESS	
AMOUNT OF MONTHLY RENT	DATE DUE

MONTH	DAY RENT RECEIVED	AMOUNT RECEIVED	AMOUNT NOT RECEIVED	LATE FEES	COMMENTS
JANUARY					
FEBRUARY					
MARCH					
APRIL					
MAY					
JUNE					
JULY					
AUGUST					
SEPTEMBER					
OCTOBER					
NOVEMBER					
DECEMBER					
TOTALS					

NOTES

RENTAL LEDGER BOOK

YEAR	
TENANT	
ADDRESS	
AMOUNT OF MONTHLY RENT	DATE DUE

MONTH	DAY RENT RECEIVED	AMOUNT RECEIVED	AMOUNT NOT RECEIVED	LATE FEES	COMMENTS
JANUARY					
FEBRUARY					
MARCH					
APRIL					
MAY					
JUNE					
JULY					
AUGUST					
SEPTEMBER					
OCTOBER					
NOVEMBER					
DECEMBER					
TOTALS					

NOTES

RENTAL LEDGER BOOK

YEAR	
TENANT	
ADDRESS	
AMOUNT OF MONTHLY RENT	DATE DUE

MONTH	DAY RENT RECEIVED	AMOUNT RECEIVED	AMOUNT NOT RECEIVED	LATE FEES	COMMENTS
JANUARY					
FEBRUARY					
MARCH					
APRIL					
MAY					
JUNE					
JULY					
AUGUST					
SEPTEMBER					
OCTOBER					
NOVEMBER					
DECEMBER					
TOTALS					

NOTES

RENTAL LEDGER BOOK

YEAR	
TENANT	
ADDRESS	
AMOUNT OF MONTHLY RENT	DATE DUE

MONTH	DAY RENT RECEIVED	AMOUNT RECEIVED	AMOUNT NOT RECEIVED	LATE FEES	COMMENTS
JANUARY					
FEBRUARY					
MARCH					
APRIL					
MAY					
JUNE					
JULY					
AUGUST					
SEPTEMBER					
OCTOBER					
NOVEMBER					
DECEMBER					
TOTALS					

NOTES

RENTAL LEDGER BOOK

YEAR	
TENANT	
ADDRESS	
AMOUNT OF MONTHLY RENT	DATE DUE

MONTH	DAY RENT RECEIVED	AMOUNT RECEIVED	AMOUNT NOT RECEIVED	LATE FEES	COMMENTS
JANUARY					
FEBRUARY					
MARCH					
APRIL					
MAY					
JUNE					
JULY					
AUGUST					
SEPTEMBER					
OCTOBER					
NOVEMBER					
DECEMBER					
TOTALS					

NOTES

RENTAL LEDGER BOOK

YEAR	
TENANT	
ADDRESS	
AMOUNT OF MONTHLY RENT	DATE DUE

MONTH	DAY RENT RECEIVED	AMOUNT RECEIVED	AMOUNT NOT RECEIVED	LATE FEES	COMMENTS
JANUARY					
FEBRUARY					
MARCH					
APRIL					
MAY					
JUNE					
JULY					
AUGUST					
SEPTEMBER					
OCTOBER					
NOVEMBER					
DECEMBER					
TOTALS					

NOTES

RENTAL LEDGER BOOK

YEAR	
TENANT	
ADDRESS	
AMOUNT OF MONTHLY RENT	DATE DUE

MONTH	DAY RENT RECEIVED	AMOUNT RECEIVED	AMOUNT NOT RECEIVED	LATE FEES	COMMENTS
JANUARY					
FEBRUARY					
MARCH					
APRIL					
MAY					
JUNE					
JULY					
AUGUST					
SEPTEMBER					
OCTOBER					
NOVEMBER					
DECEMBER					
TOTALS					

NOTES

RENTAL LEDGER BOOK

YEAR	
TENANT	
ADDRESS	
AMOUNT OF MONTHLY RENT	DATE DUE

MONTH	DAY RENT RECEIVED	AMOUNT RECEIVED	AMOUNT NOT RECEIVED	LATE FEES	COMMENTS
JANUARY					
FEBRUARY					
MARCH					
APRIL					
MAY					
JUNE					
JULY					
AUGUST					
SEPTEMBER					
OCTOBER					
NOVEMBER					
DECEMBER					
TOTALS					

NOTES

RENTAL LEDGER BOOK

YEAR	
TENANT	
ADDRESS	
AMOUNT OF MONTHLY RENT	DATE DUE

MONTH	DAY RENT RECEIVED	AMOUNT RECEIVED	AMOUNT NOT RECEIVED	LATE FEES	COMMENTS
JANUARY					
FEBRUARY					
MARCH					
APRIL					
MAY					
JUNE					
JULY					
AUGUST					
SEPTEMBER					
OCTOBER					
NOVEMBER					
DECEMBER					
TOTALS					

NOTES

RENTAL LEDGER BOOK

YEAR	
TENANT	
ADDRESS	
AMOUNT OF MONTHLY RENT	DATE DUE

MONTH	DAY RENT RECEIVED	AMOUNT RECEIVED	AMOUNT NOT RECEIVED	LATE FEES	COMMENTS
JANUARY					
FEBRUARY					
MARCH					
APRIL					
MAY					
JUNE					
JULY					
AUGUST					
SEPTEMBER					
OCTOBER					
NOVEMBER					
DECEMBER					
TOTALS					

NOTES

RENTAL LEDGER BOOK

YEAR	
TENANT	
ADDRESS	
AMOUNT OF MONTHLY RENT	DATE DUE

MONTH	DAY RENT RECEIVED	AMOUNT RECEIVED	AMOUNT NOT RECEIVED	LATE FEES	COMMENTS
JANUARY					
FEBRUARY					
MARCH					
APRIL					
MAY					
JUNE					
JULY					
AUGUST					
SEPTEMBER					
OCTOBER					
NOVEMBER					
DECEMBER					
TOTALS					

NOTES

RENTAL LEDGER BOOK

YEAR	
TENANT	
ADDRESS	
AMOUNT OF MONTHLY RENT	DATE DUE

MONTH	DAY RENT RECEIVED	AMOUNT RECEIVED	AMOUNT NOT RECEIVED	LATE FEES	COMMENTS
JANUARY					
FEBRUARY					
MARCH					
APRIL					
MAY					
JUNE					
JULY					
AUGUST					
SEPTEMBER					
OCTOBER					
NOVEMBER					
DECEMBER					
TOTALS					

NOTES

RENTAL LEDGER BOOK

YEAR	
TENANT	
ADDRESS	
AMOUNT OF MONTHLY RENT	DATE DUE

MONTH	DAY RENT RECEIVED	AMOUNT RECEIVED	AMOUNT NOT RECEIVED	LATE FEES	COMMENTS
JANUARY					
FEBRUARY					
MARCH					
APRIL					
MAY					
JUNE					
JULY					
AUGUST					
SEPTEMBER					
OCTOBER					
NOVEMBER					
DECEMBER					
TOTALS					

NOTES

RENTAL LEDGER BOOK

YEAR	
TENANT	
ADDRESS	
AMOUNT OF MONTHLY RENT	DATE DUE

MONTH	DAY RENT RECEIVED	AMOUNT RECEIVED	AMOUNT NOT RECEIVED	LATE FEES	COMMENTS
JANUARY					
FEBRUARY					
MARCH					
APRIL					
MAY					
JUNE					
JULY					
AUGUST					
SEPTEMBER					
OCTOBER					
NOVEMBER					
DECEMBER					
TOTALS					

NOTES

RENTAL LEDGER BOOK

YEAR	
TENANT	
ADDRESS	
AMOUNT OF MONTHLY RENT	DATE DUE

MONTH	DAY RENT RECEIVED	AMOUNT RECEIVED	AMOUNT NOT RECEIVED	LATE FEES	COMMENTS
JANUARY					
FEBRUARY					
MARCH					
APRIL					
MAY					
JUNE					
JULY					
AUGUST					
SEPTEMBER					
OCTOBER					
NOVEMBER					
DECEMBER					
TOTALS					

NOTES

RENTAL LEDGER BOOK

YEAR	
TENANT	
ADDRESS	
AMOUNT OF MONTHLY RENT	DATE DUE

MONTH	DAY RENT RECEIVED	AMOUNT RECEIVED	AMOUNT NOT RECEIVED	LATE FEES	COMMENTS
JANUARY					
FEBRUARY					
MARCH					
APRIL					
MAY					
JUNE					
JULY					
AUGUST					
SEPTEMBER					
OCTOBER					
NOVEMBER					
DECEMBER					
TOTALS					

NOTES

RENTAL LEDGER BOOK

YEAR	
TENANT	
ADDRESS	
AMOUNT OF MONTHLY RENT	DATE DUE	

MONTH	DAY RENT RECEIVED	AMOUNT RECEIVED	AMOUNT NOT RECEIVED	LATE FEES	COMMENTS
JANUARY					
FEBRUARY					
MARCH					
APRIL					
MAY					
JUNE					
JULY					
AUGUST					
SEPTEMBER					
OCTOBER					
NOVEMBER					
DECEMBER					
TOTALS					

NOTES

RENTAL LEDGER BOOK

YEAR	
TENANT	
ADDRESS	
AMOUNT OF MONTHLY RENT	DATE DUE

MONTH	DAY RENT RECEIVED	AMOUNT RECEIVED	AMOUNT NOT RECEIVED	LATE FEES	COMMENTS
JANUARY					
FEBRUARY					
MARCH					
APRIL					
MAY					
JUNE					
JULY					
AUGUST					
SEPTEMBER					
OCTOBER					
NOVEMBER					
DECEMBER					
TOTALS					

NOTES

RENTAL LEDGER BOOK

YEAR	
TENANT	
ADDRESS	
AMOUNT OF MONTHLY RENT	DATE DUE

MONTH	DAY RENT RECEIVED	AMOUNT RECEIVED	AMOUNT NOT RECEIVED	LATE FEES	COMMENTS
JANUARY					
FEBRUARY					
MARCH					
APRIL					
MAY					
JUNE					
JULY					
AUGUST					
SEPTEMBER					
OCTOBER					
NOVEMBER					
DECEMBER					
TOTALS					

NOTES

RENTAL LEDGER BOOK

YEAR	
TENANT	
ADDRESS	
AMOUNT OF MONTHLY RENT	DATE DUE

MONTH	DAY RENT RECEIVED	AMOUNT RECEIVED	AMOUNT NOT RECEIVED	LATE FEES	COMMENTS
JANUARY					
FEBRUARY					
MARCH					
APRIL					
MAY					
JUNE					
JULY					
AUGUST					
SEPTEMBER					
OCTOBER					
NOVEMBER					
DECEMBER					
TOTALS					

NOTES

RENTAL LEDGER BOOK

YEAR	
TENANT	
ADDRESS	
AMOUNT OF MONTHLY RENT	DATE DUE

MONTH	DAY RENT RECEIVED	AMOUNT RECEIVED	AMOUNT NOT RECEIVED	LATE FEES	COMMENTS
JANUARY					
FEBRUARY					
MARCH					
APRIL					
MAY					
JUNE					
JULY					
AUGUST					
SEPTEMBER					
OCTOBER					
NOVEMBER					
DECEMBER					
TOTALS					

NOTES

RENTAL LEDGER BOOK

YEAR	
TENANT	
ADDRESS	
AMOUNT OF MONTHLY RENT	DATE DUE

MONTH	DAY RENT RECEIVED	AMOUNT RECEIVED	AMOUNT NOT RECEIVED	LATE FEES	COMMENTS
JANUARY					
FEBRUARY					
MARCH					
APRIL					
MAY					
JUNE					
JULY					
AUGUST					
SEPTEMBER					
OCTOBER					
NOVEMBER					
DECEMBER					
TOTALS					

NOTES

RENTAL LEDGER BOOK

YEAR	
TENANT	
ADDRESS	
AMOUNT OF MONTHLY RENT	DATE DUE

MONTH	DAY RENT RECEIVED	AMOUNT RECEIVED	AMOUNT NOT RECEIVED	LATE FEES	COMMENTS
JANUARY					
FEBRUARY					
MARCH					
APRIL					
MAY					
JUNE					
JULY					
AUGUST					
SEPTEMBER					
OCTOBER					
NOVEMBER					
DECEMBER					
TOTALS					

NOTES

RENTAL LEDGER BOOK

YEAR	
TENANT	
ADDRESS	
AMOUNT OF MONTHLY RENT	DATE DUE

MONTH	DAY RENT RECEIVED	AMOUNT RECEIVED	AMOUNT NOT RECEIVED	LATE FEES	COMMENTS
JANUARY					
FEBRUARY					
MARCH					
APRIL					
MAY					
JUNE					
JULY					
AUGUST					
SEPTEMBER					
OCTOBER					
NOVEMBER					
DECEMBER					
TOTALS					

NOTES

RENTAL LEDGER BOOK

YEAR	
TENANT	
ADDRESS	
AMOUNT OF MONTHLY RENT	DATE DUE

MONTH	DAY RENT RECEIVED	AMOUNT RECEIVED	AMOUNT NOT RECEIVED	LATE FEES	COMMENTS
JANUARY					
FEBRUARY					
MARCH					
APRIL					
MAY					
JUNE					
JULY					
AUGUST					
SEPTEMBER					
OCTOBER					
NOVEMBER					
DECEMBER					
TOTALS					

NOTES

RENTAL LEDGER BOOK

YEAR	
TENANT	
ADDRESS	
AMOUNT OF MONTHLY RENT	DATE DUE

MONTH	DAY RENT RECEIVED	AMOUNT RECEIVED	AMOUNT NOT RECEIVED	LATE FEES	COMMENTS
JANUARY					
FEBRUARY					
MARCH					
APRIL					
MAY					
JUNE					
JULY					
AUGUST					
SEPTEMBER					
OCTOBER					
NOVEMBER					
DECEMBER					
TOTALS					

NOTES

Made in the USA
Middletown, DE
03 March 2024

50686398R00062